CULTURE ENCYCLOPEDIA

LITERATURE

CULTURE ENCYCLOPEDIA
LITERATURE

Antony Mason

Miles Kelly

PUBLISHING

1863589

J| 800

First published in 2002 by
Miles Kelly Publishing Ltd
The Bardfield Centre
Great Bardfield
Essex CM7 4SL

© Miles Kelly Publishing 2002

2 4 6 8 10 9 7 5 3 1

Author
Antony Mason

Designed and Edited by
Starry Dog Books

Project Editor
Belinda Gallagher

Assistant Editors
Mark Darling, Nicola Jessop, Isla Macuish

Artwork Commissioning
Lesley Cartlidge

Indexer
Jane Parker

Picture Research
Ruth Boardman, Liberty Newton

Colour Reproduction
DPI Colour, Saffron Walden, Essex

ISBN 1-84236-226-7

Printed in China

A British Library Cataloguing-in-Publication Data
A catalogue record for this book is available from the British Library

www.mileskelly.net
info@mileskelly.net

Contents

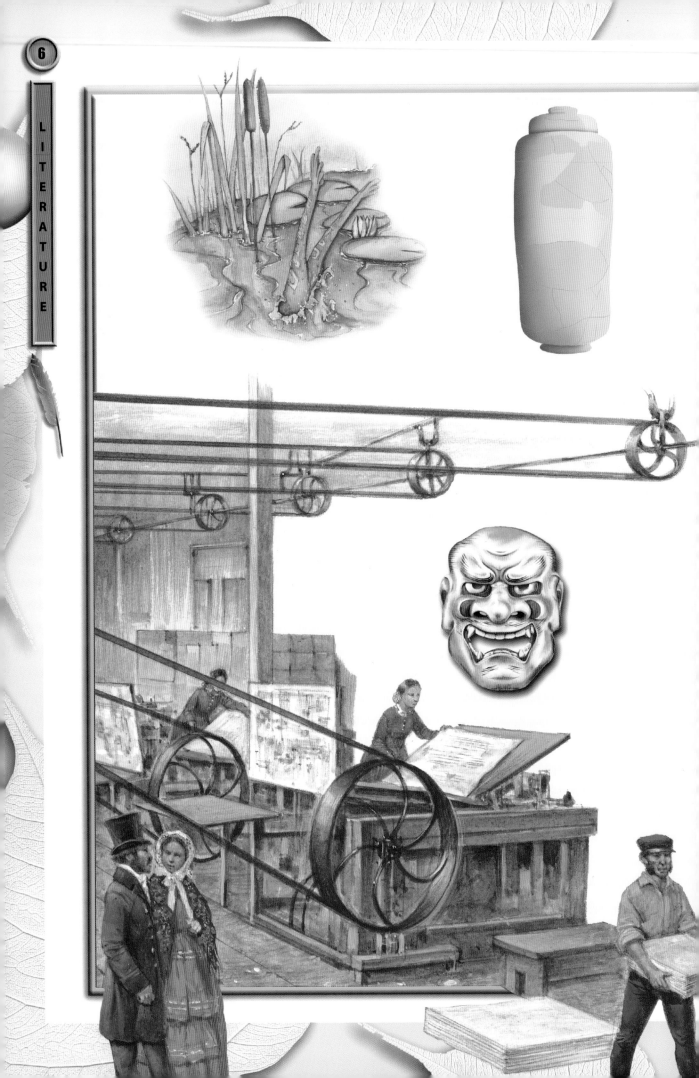

Literature

THE history of civilization dates back to just over 5000 years ago, about the same time that writing began. This is no coincidence: Writing has played a key part in the development of civilization and culture. It was used to keep records about rulers and their people – their history, religion, deeds, and laws. But it was also a way of preserving stories and ideas. Through writing, we know about myths and legends of ancient times and what ancient peoples such as the Romans did and thought, and what their imaginations produced. Writers have been adding their own contributions to literature ever since, demonstrating the extraordinary inventiveness of the human mind in stories, novels, poetry and plays.

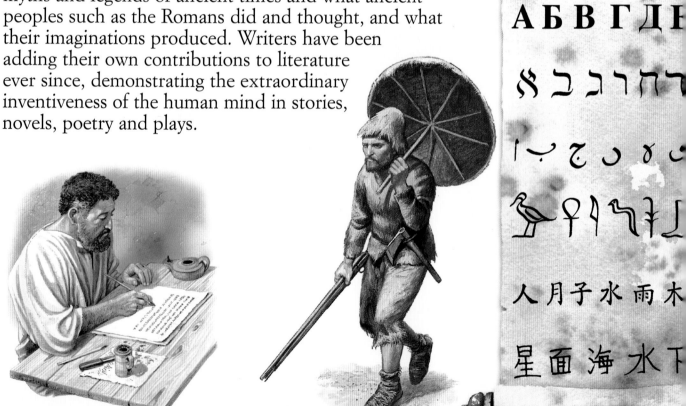

Epics and sagas

STORIES were told for thousands of years before they were written down. They were told from memory, and then passed from one generation to the next by word of mouth. Some of the earliest stories were epics – long tales in poetry that recounted the adventures of great heroes in the mythical past. To hold an audience's attention, epics had to be full of exciting events, romance, strong characters, wisdom, humour, and suspense. The long medieval tales of adventure from Norway and Iceland were called sagas.

◪ JONGLEURS AND MINSTRELS

In medieval Europe, *jongleurs* ('jugglers') put on shows in market fairs that combined juggling, acrobatics, music and poetry. They also created epic tales about knights, love and war. Minstrels entertained the rich and powerful in their castles.

◪ KING ARTHUR

Ancient legends from Britain and France tell of King Arthur and his knights. These tales of heroic deeds, love and Christian values are not just exciting stories. They also reveal how medieval knights thought they should behave according to the codes of chivalry. In the tale of King Arthur's death, his sword Excalibur is magically raised from the lake into which it has been thrown.

◪ VIKING SAGAS

The Vikings of Scandinavia and Iceland told sagas— long, exciting tales of warriors that mixed legend with true history. The sagas were created by poets called *skalds*, who made a living by telling the tales as entertainment. The sagas were not written down until long after Viking times.

◪ DANTE

The *Divine Comedy* is an epic poem of more than 14,000 lines, written by the Italian poet Dante Alighieri (1265–1321). It tells of a journey by Dante and two escorts (first the poet Virgil, then Beatrice) down to hell and up to heaven.

◩ HEROIC ADVENTURE

The epic poem *Beowulf* dates from about AD 750 and is based on Scandinavian folk tales. The hero Beowulf rids the Danes of a water monster called Grendel, and his hook-fingered mother. He becomes king, but dies killing a dragon.

THE TROJAN HORSE

Homer's great epic, the Iliad, *tells of the 10-year war between Greece and the city of Troy. According to legend, the Greek soldiers finally tricked their way into Troy by hiding inside a giant wooden horse, left, as a gift for the Trojans. Once inside the city, they opened Troy's gates to the Greek armies.*

◩ THE ARABIAN NIGHTS

Scheherazade, so the story goes, was the wife of a murderous Arab king, who kept herself alive by telling him riveting, magical stories. Many of them are very famous, such as the tales of Aladdin, Ali Baba and Sinbad the Sailor. These Arab folk tales are all at least 1000 years old.

▶ THE *ODYSSEY*

One of the world's most famous epics is the *Odyssey*. It was created in ancient Greece in about 700 BC, perhaps by a poet called Homer (no one is sure). It recounts the adventures of Odysseus on his 10-year journey home after the war against Troy. In one tragic scene, Odysseus's faithful old dog Argus dies as his master reaches his home town.

The written word

BEFORE writing was invented, all information had to be remembered and communicated as spoken words. But once writing developed, it could be stored and sent from one place to another. The Mesopotamians in the Middle East were among the first people to develop writing, in about 3400 BC. To start with, writing was used for lists, such as orders for goods sent by merchants. But soon people were writing letters, history and stories. This was the beginning of literature. The word 'literature' comes from the Latin *litteratura*, meaning writing.

◱ PICTURE-WRITING

The ancient Egyptians invented a system of writing that used more than 800 picture symbols. It was called hieroglyphics, or 'sacred carving', because it was used to write religious texts on temple walls.

◰ THE ROSETTA STONE

For centuries, Egyptian hieroglyphics were a mystery. But in 1799 a stone was found near Rosetta, in Egypt, inscribed in Egyptian, Greek, and hieroglyphics. By comparing them, scholars were able to work out what the hieroglyphics meant.

▣ ROMAN SCRIPT

Our alphabet is based on the Roman alphabet, which in turn came from the Greek alphabet. The Romans wrote in Latin, in capital letters. Latin became the language of the Christian church. Small 'lower-case' letters were invented in medieval times, as seen in this handwritten French book from the 13th century.

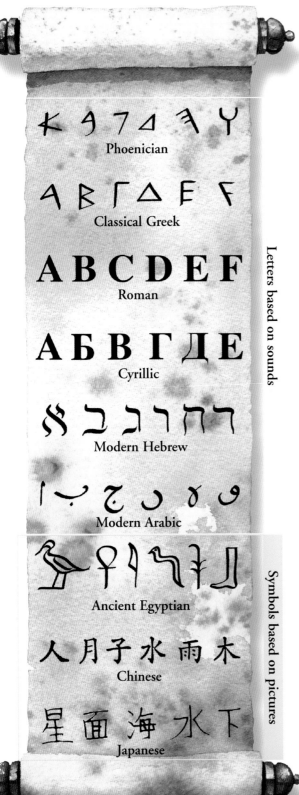

Phoenician

Classical Greek

ABCDEF
Roman

АБВГДЕ
Cyrillic

Modern Hebrew

Modern Arabic

Letters based on sounds

Ancient Egyptian

人 月 子 水 雨 木
Chinese

星 面 海 水 下
Japanese

Symbols based on pictures

◨ ALPHABET OF SOUNDS

The ancient Greeks used a system of writing based on sounds, not pictures. The advantage over picture-writing was that you could write and read any word with a set of just 24 letters, like the ones on this ancient Greek tombstone.

◧ CHINESE CHARACTERS

Chinese writing is based on pictures. Over time, the pictures became stylized into symbols, known as 'characters'. There are about 1000 basic Chinese characters, which represent a word or idea. The characters can be understood by peoples who speak different languages – they recognize the character, but pronounce it differently.

◨ LETTERS AND CHARACTERS

Sound-based alphabets can be traced back to the Phoenicians, who lived in Lebanon in ancient times. Japanese writing is based on the Chinese system, the oldest form of writing in use today.

Sacred writing

SOME of the greatest works of early literature were stories about the gods. The stories were often interwoven with historical facts. Originally they were not written down, but were passed by word of mouth from one generation to the next. The great Hindu epic the *Mahabharata* – all 220,000 lines of it – was passed down as a spoken work for over 2000 years before it was printed for the first time in the 19th century. Such sacred works are often celebrated not just for what they say, but also for the beauty and poetry of their language.

◪ HOLY BOOK OF ISLAM

Muslims believe that the Qu'ran, the holy book of Islam, contains the actual words of God as revealed to Mohammed, the prophet of Islam, after about AD 610. For this reason it is treated with great respect. Scribes copying the Qu'ran use especially beautiful forms of Arabic writing.

◪ HANDWRITTEN SCROLLS

The Jews believe that God revealed his laws to Moses on Mount Sinai, perhaps about 1200 BC. These laws form the holy book called the *Torah*, still kept in the form of large, handwritten scrolls (shown here being carried). The *Torah* is the same as the first five books of the Bible, but in a wider sense the term also covers all Jewish scriptures, laws and customs.

◪ THE DIAMOND SUTRA

The world's earliest-known printed book is a copy of the *Diamond Sutra*, a sacred Buddhist text about the perfection of wisdom, which 'cuts like a diamond'. It was printed in China in AD 868. Each page was printed from a carved woodblock, and glued together as a scroll.

DAVID AND GOLIATH

The Old Testament of the Bible contains a mixture of Jewish history, laws, teachings and folklore. One of its famous stories tells how the boy David (later a great king) bravely took on the giant Philistine warrior Goliath and killed him with a well-aimed slingshot.

◪ SAINT PAUL

When it started, Christianity was a Jewish movement. Saint Paul preached its message to non-Jews across the Roman Empire. His teaching is preserved in the Bible as a collection of letters, called Epistles, to the new Christian communities.

◪ SCRIPTURE OF THE SIKHS

The main scripture of the Sikhs is called *Adi Granth*, or 'First Book', a collection of nearly 6000 hymns of the Sikh gurus, or religious teachers. They were written down between 1604 and 1704. The book is also known as *Guru Granth Sahib*, because it is treated as if it were a living guru.

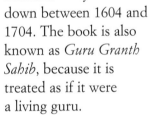

THE DEAD SEA SCROLLS

The Bible was preserved through the ages in handwritten copies. In 1947, 2000-year-old scrolls of the Old Testament books were found near the Dead Sea in Israel, stored in pots. They are much older than other known copies.

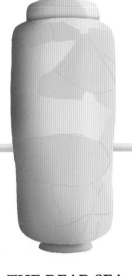

The printing revolution

UNTIL about 600 years ago there were very few books, and they were expensive. Almost all books in Europe were written by hand, each one taking months to produce. Only educated and rich people used them. But in about 1438, Johannes Gutenberg invented an efficient way of printing, using 'movable type'. Suddenly it was possible to mass-produce books in large numbers, and quite cheaply. More people began to read, and soon newspapers, pamphlets and posters were being printed, too.

◨ WOODBLOCK PRINTING
In woodblock printing, which dates back to 9th-century-AD China, each page is separately carved. The Japanese continued to use this method, as seen in this print of about 1850.

◧ THE PRINTING INDUSTRY
By 1850, in Europe and the United States, large printing workshops – like this one in Boston – were printing and assembling thousands of copies of illustrated books and magazines in just a few days. The new steam-powered rotary presses, introduced in 1846, could print 8000 sheets an hour.

◪ HERBERT INGRAM
The first magazine to use lots of pictures was the *Illustrated London News*, founded as a 'weekly' by Herbert Ingram in 1842. The pictures were printed from engravings on metal plates. After the 1880s, photographs were used.

◪ NEWSPAPER PRINTING

Newspapers today are printed on machines
called web presses. Paper is fed from huge rolls
through the press at a rate of up to 1000 metres
a minute. The pages are then folded and cut,
ready for distribution.

GUTENBERG

*In about 1438, the German Johannes
Gutenberg developed a way of printing
using 'movable type'. First he cast
hundreds of individual metal letters in
moulds. Then he arranged these letters
into pages of
text, which he
printed on a
press – a far
quicker
method
than
woodblock
printing.*

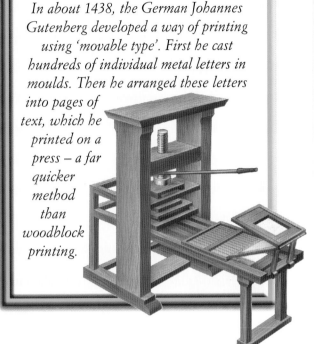

◁ PROPAGANDA

Printing is a good way of spreading information.
Millions of copies of a document can be made
quickly. Of course, the information may be true
or false. Governments print 'propaganda'–
pro-government literature – to win support,
such as this poster produced by the Chinese
Communists when they came to power at the
end of a civil war in 1949.

▷ COLOUR PRINTING

If you look at a printed colour picture under a
magnifying glass, you will see a mass of tiny dots. The
colour is actually made up of just four different printing
inks: yellow, cyan (blue),
magenta (red) and black.
Each colour is applied by
a separate roller as the
paper passes through the
printing press.

| yellow | cyan | magenta | black |

The novel: Early classics

DURING the 15th century, collections of stories, such as Boccaccio's *Decameron*, became popular in Europe. The collections were called 'novels', from the Italian word *novella*, meaning a piece of news or a tale. By 1605 the novel had developed into a long, imaginary tale with one or more central characters, but it was not until the 18th century that the novel became a popular form of entertainment. As more people learned to read, printing increased and readers were able buy their own copies of imaginary worlds.

◪ PRINCE GENJI

The Tale of Genji is thought to be the world's oldest full-length novel. It was written about AD 1000 by Murasaki Shikibu, a lady-in-waiting to the empress of Japan. It tells the story of Prince Genji and his various loves.

◧ DOSTOEVSKY

Russia has produced some of the world's greatest novelists. Feodor Dostoevsky (1821–81) is famous for novels such as *Crime and Punishment*, *The Idiot* and *The Brothers Karamazov*. Although they deal with serious subjects such as prisons, madness and murder, they also sparkle with humour and a sense of the absurd, and contain brilliantly drawn characters. Dostoevsky had a major influence on the development of modern literature.

DEFOE AND SELKIRK

Daniel Defoe's Robinson Crusoe *was based on the story of a real-life castaway. In 1704 a Scottish sailor named Alexander Selkirk (left) was stranded on an island off Chile. Five years passed before he was rescued.*

◪ CHARLES DICKENS – COMIC GENIUS

The novels of Charles Dickens (1812–70) were hugely popular. Set in the industrial world of Victorian England, they are filled with larger-than-life characters. In *A Christmas Carol*, the miserly Scrooge is haunted by ghosts who reveal to him the damaging effects of his meanness.

▶ TOM SAWYER

Some characters from novels have become world famous. *The Adventures of Tom Sawyer*, by American author Mark Twain (1835–1910), tells the story of a mischievous but engaging boy growing up in Missouri, USA. Numerous film versions have been made, including this one from 1938.

◤ JANE AUSTEN

Novels do not have to tell of great events or adventures. Jane Austen (1775–1817) was a genius at portraying the lives of ordinary people in a carefully observed way and with wry humor. Her novels include *Sense and Sensibility, Emma* and *Pride and Prejudice*.

◤ DON QUIXOTE, GALLANT HERO

When the first part of *Don Quixote de la Mancha* was published in 1605, it was an immediate bestseller. It is often said to be the first 'modern' novel. Written by the Spanish author Miguel de Cervantes (1547–1616), it follows the adventures of Don Quixote, an aging gentleman who mistakenly believes he is a knight living in the Age of Chivalry.

THE HUNCHBACK OF NOTRE DAME

Victor Hugo (1802–85) was one of the most famous of all French writers, celebrated for his poems and many novels. Perhaps his most famous novel is The Hunchback of Notre Dame, *in which he shows humans to be a blend of good and evil. The hunchback is Quasimodo, an outcast in the cathedral bell tower, who is shown kindness only by the woman he is sent to capture.*

The novel: Traditions

DURING the 19th century, writers began to explore the storytelling possibilities of the novel. They learned to combine intriguing characters with inventive plots, and used their imaginary worlds to make comments on the real world around them. Various types of novel developed, such as history novels, thrillers, detective novels and romantic novels. Novels have remained one of the most popular forms of literature ever since. They have been translated into numerous languages, and many of them are made into films.

◪ SCHINDLER'S ARK

Some novels are closely based on historical fact, like this novel by the Australian writer Thomas Keneally (born 1935). It tells the story of Oskar Schindler, a German who saved more than 1300 Jews from certain death in Nazi camps in Poland.

◪ WAR AND PEACE

Count Leo Tolstoy (1829–1910) was one of the greatest Russian novelists, as well as a playwright and philosopher who developed his own form of Christianity. He is most famous for his epic novel *War and Peace*. Set against the war with France under Napoleon (this scene is from the 1956 film version), it explains Tolstoy's view that history is chaotic and has no pattern.

DETECTIVE NOVELS

'The Murders in the Rue Morgue' *by the American writer Edgar Allan Poe (1809–49) was probably the first detective story – one of the most popular forms of fiction. The most famous detective, often mistaken for a real person, was Sherlock Holmes, created by the British writer Arthur Conan Doyle (1859–1930).*

☑ GARCÍA MÁRQUEZ

In the 1940s, a new kind of writing emerged from Latin America. Called 'magic realism', it mixed reality with imaginative fantasy.

One of the best-known books in this style is *One Hundred Years of Solitude* by the Colombian writer Gabriel García Márquez (born 1928). In 1982 he won the Nobel Prize for Literature.

◀ THE BRONTË SISTERS

The three Brontë sisters, Charlotte, Emily, and Anne, wrote some of the greatest novels of early Victorian England, and were a major influence on later novel writing. Much of their work is about human relationships and the powerful forces of love. Charlotte (1816–55) is most famous for *Jane Eyre* (shown here); Emily (1818–48) for *Wuthering Heights*; and Anne (1820–49) for *The Tenant of Wildfell Hall*.

☑ SALMAN RUSHDIE

Novels can contain ideas so strong that they provoke anger and fear. After the British novelist Salman Rushdie (born 1947) published *The Satanic Verses* in 1988, it was condemned as blasphemous (offensive to God) by the Muslim religious authorities in Iran. He has lived under the threat of assassination by religious fanatics ever since.

◢ JAMES BOND

One of the world's best-known fictional characters is James Bond, the secret service agent at the centre of a series of spy thrillers by the British novelist Ian Fleming (1908–64). All twelve of Fleming's Bond novels were made into films, five of them starring Sean Connery (shown here).

Poetry: Different kinds

SOME poems are very long, some very short. Some tell long and complicated stories, like the great epics of Homer. Others paint pictures of a brief moment. In some poems all the lines rhyme; others have no rhyming lines at all. In fact, it is not easy to say what poetry is exactly. But most poetry is written out in lines, while novels and short stories are written in continuous text, or 'prose'. Poetry also tends to use language inventively. The poet brings together language and ideas to say something new and memorable about the world.

◨ POETIC TALES
Geoffrey Chaucer (*c.*1345–1400) was the first great poet to write in English. His most famous work is *The Canterbury Tales*, a collection of 23 stories in verse told by a group of characters as they travel to Canterbury. Dramatic, romantic, touching, hilarious – together they paint a vivid picture of life in 14th-century England.

◩ JAPANESE HAIKU
The Japanese developed a very short type of non-rhyming poem called a haiku, usually just 17 syllables long, written as three lines (divided as 5-7-5 syllables). The aim was to capture a moment of intense perception, often linking a detail of nature with a sense of eternity. Here is an example from the poet Bashō (1644–94), a master of haiku:

Furuike ya, kawazu tobikomu, mizu no oto.

> *Breaking the silence*
> *Of an ancient pond,*
> *A frog jumped into*
> *water – a deep*
> *resonance.*

◪ BALLADS
Originally ballads were popular songs written to accompany a dance. As poems, they usually tell a dramatic story using strong rhythm and rhyme. In the 15th and 16th centuries, many ballads were written about the legendary outlaw of Sherwood Forest, Robin Hood, and his band of men.

POEMS OF LOVE AND LIBERTY

The French poet and novelist Victor Hugo (1802–1885) is best rememberd by the French for his poetry. His expressive use of language clearly portrayed his belief in liberty and his understanding of human suffering. Hugo was also a great romantic poet and this was firmly established by the publication of *The Orientals* in 1829.

CHILDREN'S POETRY

Young children love the musical sound of poetry. British writer A. A. Milne (1882–1956) – famous as the author of the stories about the bear Winnie-the-Pooh – wrote numerous funny poems for children. His two famous collections are: When We Were Very Young *and* Now We Are Six.

POWERFUL IMAGES

Through the intensity of their language, poems are able to convey strong images of an imaginary world to the reader. In his famous long poem *The Rime of the Ancient Mariner,* the British poet Samuel Taylor Coleridge (1772–1834) paints a vivid picture of despair on board a ship cursed with bad luck after the mariner shoots an albatross, a seabird.

THE ROMANTIC VIEW OF NATURE

In the late 18th century, a group of British poets gathered in the beautiful Lake District of northwest England and wrote about their feelings for nature. William Wordsworth (1770–1850), Robert Southey (1774–1843), and Samuel Taylor Coleridge became known as the 'Lake Poets'. They had a major influence on the way people looked at nature.

Poetry: Poetic heroes

BECAUSE of the original way they see and describe the world, poets have held a special place in society since ancient times. Often in the past, they had an important influence on the way people viewed the world. Poets are concerned to capture in words people's feelings about all kinds of subjects – from love and death, to feelings about their country, or nature, or just the small things in everyday life. Or they might convey a powerful vision of a spiritual world beyond our daily lives. Some of the most successful poets became superstars in their day, and are celebrated as national heroes.

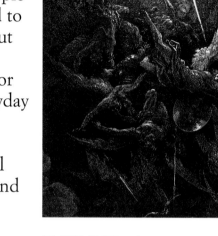

◩ HEAVEN AND HELL

The English poet John Milton (1608–74) wrote numerous poems, as well as pamphlets about the church and government. In the 1650s he went blind and had to dictate his work, including his great epic *Paradise Lost*. This tells how the angel Satan rebelled against God, who threw him out of Heaven.

◩ LORD BYRON

The English aristocrat George Gordon, Lord Byron (1788–1824), lived and died the life of a heroic Romantic poet. He became a celebrity across Europe after the publication of his long narrative poem *Childe Harold's Pilgrimage*. Byron died of fever while fighting to liberate the Greeks from Turkish rule.

GARCÍA LORCA

Writing with an intense feeling for his country, Federico García Lorca (1898–1938) became the best-known poet of his day in Spain. His poems often explore the theme of violent death. Lorca himself was shot by nationalist soldiers just before the outbreak of the Spanish Civil War.

▭ 'SEASON OF MISTS...'

John Keats (1795–1821) is one of the greatest English poets, celebrated for his rich imagery. He wrote both narrative verse and 'lyric' poems such as odes, which are short and expressive of feelings or sensations. Autumn, for example, he describes as a 'season of mists and mellow fruitfulness...'. Keats died of tuberculosis, aged just 25.

◩ ELIZABETH BARRETT BROWNING

In 1844, *Poems* made Elizabeth Barrett (1806–61) one of the best-known poets in England. She married the poet Robert Browning (1812–89), and they lived mainly in Italy. She was celebrated for her love poems, and her outspoken opinions about politics, slavery and women in society.

▭ MARINA TSVETAYEVA

Marina Tsvetayeva (1892–1941) was one of Russia's greatest poets of the 20th century. She opposed the Communist Revolution of 1917 and left Russia in 1922, but still wrote lovingly of her homeland. She returned in 1939, but was forced to leave Moscow during World War II. Lonely and isolated, she committed suicide.

◪ YEVGENY ONEGIN

Aleksandr Sergeyevich Pushkin (1799–1837) is Russia's most celebrated and beloved poet, and is known as the founder of Russian literature. His greatest work, *Yevgeny Onegin*, is a novel in verse. It was made into an opera by the Russian composer Tchaikovsky (a set from the opera is shown here). Pushkin died age 37 after fighting a duel.

Drama

PLAYWRITING is one of the oldest forms of literature. Plays written 2500 years ago by the ancient Greek dramatist Aeschylus are still performed today. The greatest plays capture the imagination of the spectators and can make them sit on the edge of their seats with fear or excitement, or cry with laughter or emotion. But a good play depends on more than just the written words – it needs good actors to interpret them and scenery, costumes and lighting to add to the drama.

◥ CLASSICAL THEATRE

In ancient times plays were a hugely popular form of entertainment. In Europe the tradition began in Greece, and was later adopted by the Romans. Open-air theatres such as this Roman theatre at Jarash in Jordan held as many as 15,000 people.

◤ *FAUST*

The greatest figure in German literature is Johann Wolfgang von Goethe (1749–1832), poet, playwright and scientist. One of his most famous works is the two-part drama *Faust*, which tells the story of a scholar who sells his soul to the devil (seen here in a 1926 film version).

◀ A NEW KIND OF PLAY

The Russian playwright Anton Chekhov (1860–1904) helped to shape modern drama. He was more interested in exploring the interaction of his characters' thoughts and emotions than in devising an eventful plot. This scene is from a film version of *The Three Sisters*.

◪ *NŌ* DRAMA

Japanese *Nō* drama dates
back to the 14th century. Male
actors, often in masks like this one,
chant the words and dance to music in
a highly stylized performance, which has been
fixed by hundreds of years of tradition. *Nō*
theatre was intended for aristocratic audiences,
while another form of traditional Japanese
theatre, *Kabuki*, was for ordinary people.

◪ SHAKESPEARE

One of the most
celebrated writers
ever is the English
playwright and poet
William Shakespeare (1564–1616). He wrote
some 37 plays, including many of the classics of
theatre, such as the tragedies *Othello, Macbeth*
and *Romeo and Juliet* and the comedy
A Midsummer Night's Dream. The huge success
of the 1998 film *Shakespeare in Love* (shown
above) suggests that people's fascination for
Shakespeare and his plays is very much alive.

◪ THEATRE OF IDEAS

The German playwright Bertolt Brecht (1898–
1956) believed that plays should change the way
people think. He thought that audiences would
understand the message better if they were
constantly reminded that they were watching a
play, not reality. Among his best-known plays is
The Caucasian Chalk Circle (shown here), which
questions motherly love in a dispute over a child.

OSCAR WILDE

*The brilliantly witty Irish writer Oscar
Wilde (1854–1900) shot to fame and
fortune with his comic plays, notably* The
Importance of Being Earnest, *which
commented on the social 'manners' of the
time. Wilde was famous for his showy,
artistic behaviour and
looks – he wore a
green carnation in
his buttonhole on
the opening night of
his plays. But after
three famous trials, he
died in exile in Paris.*

Non-fiction

NOVELS and short stories are described as 'fiction' – they portray imaginary worlds. The opposite is 'non-fiction' – books about real things, activities, people or events. Books on history, science, geography, religion, gardening, cooking, nature, art, and sport, are all non-fiction. Reference books such as these, and encyclopedias and dictionaries, must be precise, accurate and easy to understand. History, biographies of famous people and travel books have to be factually correct, yet also well written to hold their readers' attention.

◪ DICTIONARIES
The earliest dictionaries simply listed foreign words and their meanings. But in 1755, Dr Samuel Johnson (1709–84) defined the words of his own language, in his *Dictionary of the English Language*.

◪ KEEPING A RECORD
By keeping diaries and letters, writers have provided the world with important information and opinions about events that happened in their lifetime. Samuel Pepys (1633–1703), an English government official in London, kept a diary from 1660 to 1669. As well as details of his personal life, it records eyewitness accounts of major events, such as the Great Fire of London of 1666, shown in this painting.

HISTORY
The ancient Greeks developed the art of history writing and passed it on to the Romans. Julius Caesar (c.100–44 BC) was not just a brilliant Roman general and leader, but a great war historian.

◪ TRAVEL WRITING
Some of the most fascinating non-fiction recounts explorers' adventures through strange lands. The great Norwegian polar explorer Roald Amundsen (1878–1928) described his famous journey in 1911 in his book *The South Pole*.

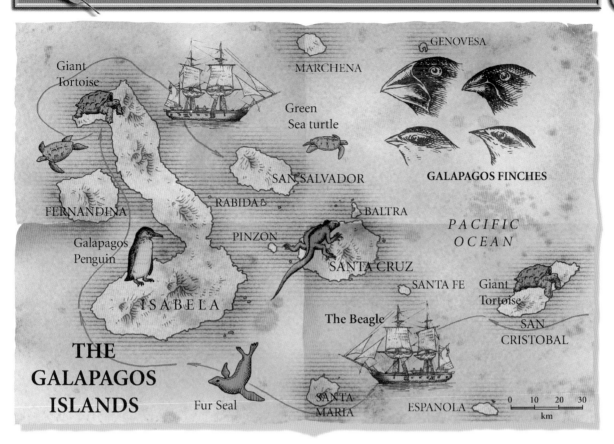

GENOVESA
MARCHENA
Giant
Tortoise
Green
Sea turtle
SAN SALVADOR
GALAPAGOS FINCHES
RABIDA
FERNANDINA
BALTRA
Galapagos
Penguin
PINZON
*PACIFIC
OCEAN*
SANTA CRUZ
SANTA FE   Giant
Tortoise
I S A B E L A
The Beagle
SAN
CRISTOBAL
**THE
GALAPAGOS
ISLANDS**
Fur Seal
SANTA
MARIA
ESPANOLA
0   10   20   30
km

BIG NEW IDEAS

When the young British scientist Charles Darwin (1809–82)
visited the Galapagos Islands, off South America, in
1835, he noticed how the animals had
adapted physically to suit the conditions on
each island. This helped him to formulate his
theory of evolution, published in *The Origin of
Species* (1859),
a book that
changed the
way we look
at the history
of life on Earth.

water vapour
condenses,
forming
water
droplets

plants give
off water

BOOKS FOR
LEARNING

Making information
interesting and fun to
learn is a major challenge.
The information has to be
clear and well presented.
Illustrations drawn to go with
the text, such as this diagram of
the water cycle, can help explain
a difficult subject. A 'glossary'
explains terms and an index allows
readers to find a subject quickly.

water from oceans
and lakes
evaporates

ANNE FRANK'S DIARY

Anne Frank (1929–45) was a
German Jewish girl who, during
Word War II, spent two
years hiding with her
family from the Nazis
in a secret apartment
in Amsterdam. In
1944 they were
betrayed, and Anne died in
Belsen concentration camp. Her
diary is one of the most vivid documents
about the suffering inflicted by the Nazi regime.

Children's books

SOME of the most famous works of literature written during the 19th and 20th centuries were written for children. Authors who successfully capture a child's imagination can lead the reader into extraordinary imaginary worlds – children's books are often more inventive than adult fiction. Pictures, or illustrations, can also help to fire the imagination and can play a large part in the success of children's books. Pictures in the original *Alice in Wonderland* were by the illustrator John Tenniel (1820–1914).

☑ STORIES WITH MORALS

Fables are stories that feature animals who behave like humans, and give a clear moral lesson. In *The Hare and the Tortoise*, a fable by Aesop (an ancient Greek writer who lived about 620 to 560 BC), the speedy, boastful hare is so confident of winning a race against the tortoise that he goes to sleep. The slow-but-steady tortoise wins the race!

◁ FAIRY TALES

The son of a poor shoemaker, storyteller Hans Christian Andersen (1805–75) became Denmark's most famous author, known above all for his fairy tales. He wrote more than 150 in all, including *The Ugly Duckling*, *The Snow Queen*, and *The Wild Swans* (shown here).

☑ ALICE IN WONDERLAND

To amuse 10-year-old Alice Liddell and her sisters, Lewis Carroll (1832–98) – a mathematics teacher at Oxford University – invented a series of strange and fanciful stories, published as *Alice's Adventures in Wonderland* and *Through the Looking Glass*. Here, Alice is having tea with the Mad Hatter and his friends.

TREASURE ISLAND

One of the most memorable characters in children's fiction is Long John Silver, the one-legged pirate in Treasure Island, *by British author Robert Louis Stevenson (1850–94). He nearly succeeds in cheating the boy hero Jim Hawkins in the quest to recover the buried treasure.*

◪ THE WIZARD OF OZ

The Wonderful Wizard of Oz, written in 1899 by American Frank L. Baum (1856–1919), is a fairy tale about finding your heart's desire: courage, brains, a heart and home. It was made into a hugely successful film in 1939.

◪ COLLECTORS OF FAIRY TALES

Many of the most famous fairy tales were folk stories that have been collected and retold. The French poet Charles Perrault (1628–1703) made popular such favourites as *Cinderella* (shown here) and *Sleeping Beauty*. Other favourites, including *Hansel and Gretel*, were collected by the German brothers Jakob (1785–1863) and Wilhelm Grimm (1786–1859).

◪ WILLIE WONKA

Charlie and the Chocolate Factory is one of the funny and imaginative books by British author Roald Dahl (1916–90). The film version was renamed *Willie Wonka and the Chocolate Factory.*

Science fiction

DURING the 19th century, people started to speculate as to how science and new technology might change the world. Authors such as Jules Verne and H.G. Wells wrote stories about future worlds equipped with new machines. This kind of writing has now developed into the specialized field of writing called science fiction. And, just as science and technology have become infinitely more complex and sophisticated since the 19th century, so too has science fiction.

H.G.WELLS'
WAR OF THE WORLDS

Color by **Technicolor**

A MIGHTY PANORAMA OF EARTH-SHAKING FURY!

TWO YEARS IN THE MAKING!

NOTHING SO SPECTACULAR EVER PUT ON FILM BEFORE!

PRODUCED BY **GEORGE PAL** WHO GAVE YOU 'DESTINATION MOON' & 'WHEN WORLDS COLLIDE'

Paramount Presents **THE WAR OF THE WORLDS** Color by TECHNICOLOR
Produced by GEORGE PAL · Directed by BYRON HASKIN · Screenplay by BARRÉ LYNDON · Based on the Novel by H. G. Wells

�« ▪ FATHER OF SCIENCE FICTION

The first writer to bring futuristic science to novels was the French author Jules Verne (1828–1905). His books centred on travel adventures, notably *Journey to the Centre of the Earth* (this scene is from the 1959 film version) and *Twenty Thousand Leagues under the Sea*.

◀ H.G. WELLS

British author Herbert George Wells (1866–1946) believed that advances in science might create a better world. He wrote a series of highly successful science-fiction novels, such as *The First Men in the Moon* and *The Time Machine*. In *The War of the Worlds* (made into a film in 1953), he envisaged Martians invading Earth and landing in the United States.

◀ *BRAVE NEW WORLD*

A nightmarish vision of the future was created by British novelist Aldous Huxley (1894–1963) in *Brave New World* (this scene is from the US TV series). In a 25th-century world, humans are hatched in incubators and lead trouble-free lives, at the cost of all individual freedom.

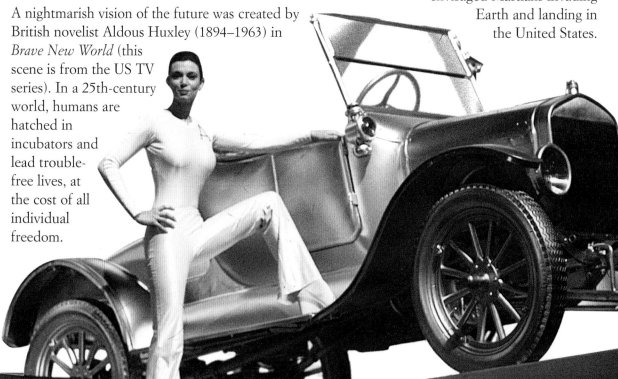

2001: A SPACE ODYSSEY

The British science-fiction author Arthur C. Clarke (b. 1917) made some remarkable predictions, including satellite communication. The 1968 film *2001: A Space Odyssey* (pictured below), based on his screenplay and short story, includes many predictions, such as interplanetary space travel and a talking, intelligent computer.

ISAAC ASIMOV

A key figure in the development of science fiction was the Russian-born American writer and biochemist, Isaac Asimov (1920–92). He is best known for his Foundation *trilogy, written in the early 1950s, which traces the collapse and revival of a futuristic interstellar empire. Asimov wrote some 500 books in total, including many books on science.*

THE FIRST ROBOTS

The word 'robot' (from the Czech word for forced labour) was invented in 1920 by the Czech novelist and playwright Karel Čapek (1890–1938). In his play *R.U.R. (Rossum's Universal Robots)*, a scientist invents human-like machines that come to dominate the world and threaten to wipe out the human race. Today people can make their own robots, like this 'Mindstorms' toy.

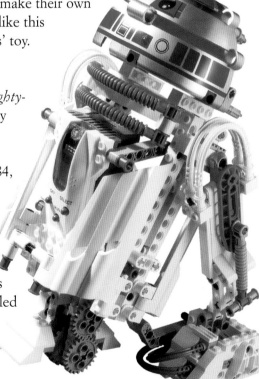

BIG BROTHER

The novel *Nineteen Eighty-Four,* written in 1948 by British author George Orwell (1903–50), and made into a film in 1984, gave the world a frightening vision of the future (now our past!). It describes a Britain where all independent thought is monitored and controlled by the government: 'Big Brother is watching you'.

The power of the word

SOME books carry such a powerful message that they have the power to change the course of history. The ideas of the German philosopher Karl Marx (1818–83), published in *The Communist Manifesto* and *Das Kapital*, for example, resulted in several revolutions and transformed the lives of millions of people around the world. On a smaller scale, Arthur Conan Doyle's descriptions of analyzing crime scenes – in his novels about the fictional detective Sherlock Holmes – had an important influence on police methods and detective work at the beginning of the 20th century.

◪ THE TRUTH ABOUT WORLD WAR I

During World War I, soldiers lived in wretched conditions in the trenches that faced each other along the Western Front in France and Belgium. Thousands died in single battles. Their families knew little of this horror until it was described in 1929 in *All Quiet on the Western Front*, a novel by the German writer Erich Maria Remarque (1898–1970).

◪ UNCLE TOM'S CABIN

Slavery was part of life in the Southern states until the American Civil War of 1861–65. The cruelty of slavery had been exposed in the novel *Uncle Tom's Cabin* by the writer Harriet Beecher Stowe (1811–96). Published in 1852, the book played a major part in encouraging opposition to slavery.

◪ GULLIVER'S TRAVELS

The fantasy-adventure story about Gulliver in the lands of miniature people and giants, by the British author Jonathan Swift (1667–1745), is a witty satire on human foolishness. It mocks the words and deeds of politicians, scientists and philosophers.

CRY, THE BELOVED COUNTRY

In 1948, the first novel by the South African writer Alan Paton (1903–88) brought to world attention the cruelty and injustices of 'apartheid'. This official government policy separated people of different races in South Africa, and limited the rights of the majority black population. A film version was made in 1995.

THE GRAPES OF WRATH

During the 1930s, a drought in the American Midwest turned much of the farmland into a 'Dust Bowl'. Ruined farmers fled to California, where they took up work as fruit pickers. *The Grapes of Wrath,* by the American writer John Steinbeck (1902–68), aroused much public sympathy for their hardship and misery. The book was made into a film in 1940.

BLACK BEAUTY

This popular children's book by the British author Anna Sewell (1820–78) is about a beautiful black horse that suffers in cruel hands before eventually finding a happy home. It helped in improving the way people in Britain treated their horses.

MAO'S 'LITTLE RED BOOK'

During the 1960s, some 800 million copies of the *Quotations from Chairman Mao* were distributed to everyone in China. These words of wisdom from Mao-Zedong (1893–1976), the Chinese Communist leader, inspired fanatical support for Mao during his 'Cultural Revolution'. However, the revolution turned out to be a political disaster.

Publishing

BOOKS remain a key source of information and entertainment in our world. Hundreds of thousands of new books are published every year. Almost all of them are produced by publishing companies. Publishers select the best books from among the many that authors send to them, or they commission authors to write books for them. The Internet will bring big changes to the world of books; new kinds of literature may develop, perhaps combining music and film. But these too will have to entertain their audience successfully and hold its attention, just as the old storytellers did when literature first began.

◢ BESTSELLERS

The bestselling book of all time is the Bible. Over the centuries, about 6 billion copies of the Bible have been sold. The aim of most publishers is to create bestsellers!

◩ AUTHORS

Authors are the starting point for most books. Before they start writing, they may spend many weeks researching their subject and making notes on how to shape the content of the book. Some write out their work by hand, others use a computer, and they often make many revisions along the way. Most authors agree that writing is: '10 percent inspiration and 90 percent hard work'.

◧ EDITORS AND DESIGNERS

At the publisher's office, an editor goes through the author's text, correcting any errors, making suggestions for changes, and questioning anything that is not clear. A designer plans how the pages will look. He or she chooses the size and style for the type, and for illustrated books works out where to position the pictures and text so that they are closely linked. The designer also briefs the illustrator on what the pictures need to show.

◪ ILLUSTRATORS

Book illustrators are artists who specialize in turning ideas into visual images. They generally work on books of a particular kind, for example children's storybooks, reference books like this one, or complex scientific publications. Following the designer's instructions, the illustrator usually produces pencil sketches (called 'roughs') first, for approval, before painting the final illustrations.

E-BOOKS

Novels and other electronic books (e-books) can be downloaded from the Internet to your home computer. Soon it may be possible to read them on portable, booklike screens. We may be on the threshold of an entirely new age of literature.

◪ PRINTING

Before a book is printed, the pages are sent in electronic form to a 'reproduction house', where they are made into films. Some printers now print from electronic files instead of films. This method of printing is called CTP (Computer to Plate). The printer prepares metal plates which are attached to rollers. These are inked, and large sheets of paper are run through the machine (shown here). The sheets are then folded, trimmed and bound.

◪ BOOKSHOPS AND LIBRARIES

Printed books are stored in a publisher's warehouse. Booksellers and libraries order the books they want to stock from the publisher. Bookshops choose books that they think will appeal to their bookbuyers. Libraries hold a greater range of information and learning, and are an key element of the civilized world.

Glossary

APARTHEID
The policy once held by the South African government that kept black people separate from white people and gave them fewer human rights, to keep white people in power.

ASSASSINATION
The murder of a person such as a religious leader, politician or state leader, usually for supposed political or religious reasons.

BIOGRAPHIES
Accounts of a person's life, written or told by someone else.

BLASPHEMOUS
Anything considered to cause offence to God or a deity, such as irreverent words spoken or written about a religious subject.

CASTAWAY
A person who survives a disaster, especially a shipwreck, and who reaches a strange, remote land, where he or she must survive until rescued.

CHIVALRY
Religious, moral and social rules of behaviour, which medieval knights were supposed to follow. Today it refers to polite, courteous behaviour, especially of men towards women.

COMMISSION
To order a picture or other piece of work to be created, often especially for and to the instructions of the person making the order.

COMMUNIST
A member of a political party which supports a system where all buildings, factories, fields and other property are publicly owned. Each person is provided for according to his or her needs.

CURSED
When someone has become the subject of an evil or hurtful spell, magical wish or supernatural power and is in danger of harm.

DETECTIVE
A person, often from a police force, trained to find the causes of crimes and the people who did them, by searching for and analyzing clues, questioning suspects and similar methods.

DICTATE
In one meaning, to give orders which others cannot question or refuse; powerful people called dictators do this. In another meaning, to speak or read aloud so that the words can be written down or otherwise recorded.

DUEL
A contest or battle between two people, especially a formal contest in historical times between two gentlemen, to settle an argument, respond to a challenge or repay an insult. The contest involved pistols or swords and often resulted in serious injury or death.

ENGRAVING
A printing technique where a pattern or image is cut, or engraved, into a metal or wooden plate, ink is rubbed on, and then the plate is pressed onto paper.

EPIC
A long story, poem or tale, which tells of many great and magnificent deeds, especially involving a hero or heroine.

EVOLUTION
How animals and plants change gradually over time, by the process called natural selection, and become better suited or adapted to their environment.

FABLES
Short stories, often based on animal characters, which teach lessons especially to children, to show them how they can lead better lives.

FANATICS
People whose enthusiasm for something, possibly a religion, hobby or sport, becomes stronger than ordinary people's would be, and perhaps causes problems.

FOLK-TALE
A traditional story, based on fact or imagination, which is part of the history of a group of people, and which is passed down from generation to generation, usually by word of mouth.

HEROES AND HEROINES
Men and women who are the main characters in a story, often showing great courage, strength and cleverness, so that they save others from misfortune. They are usually very good-looking too.

HIEROGLYPHS
A system of writing which uses small pictures to represent words, syllables or sounds, and which was invented and used by the ancient Egyptians for their religious texts.

INCUBATORS
Machines that keep objects in a compartment at a certain constant temperature, especially to keep living things warm, such as eggs or babies.

KNIGHTS
Soldiers or noble people of medieval times who were armed with swords, lances and shields, who wore metal suits of armour, and who rode on strong war horses to fight for their lord, king or country.

LEAGUE
An old measure of distance, used especially by sailors and explorers – one league was equal to about three miles or five kilometres.

LEGEND
A popular traditional story or myth, about historical characters and past events, for which there is no modern proof that it is true.

MARTIANS
Living beings from the planet Mars, which is thought to be the most likely place where life might exist – but so far, no evidence of any Martians has been found.

MEDIEVAL
Usually referring to the Middle or Dark Ages, a 1000-year period in history, which generally began at the end of the Roman era, around 400 AD, and ended with the Renaissance, around 1400 AD.

MESOPOTAMIA
The region between the Tigris and Euphrates rivers, which is now parts of Iraq, Syria and Turkey. Some of the world's early civilizations were based there, such as the Sumerians more than 7000 years ago.

MINSTRELS
Entertainers of historical times who usually sang and played musical instruments; some were given permanent positions or jobs in the households of the rich.

NAZI
Member of the German National Socialist Workers' Party, an organization with extreme views on race, power and many other subjects, which took control of Germany in 1933 under its dictator, Adolf Hitler.

NOBEL PRIZES
Six international awards given annually to people who have made great achievements in physics, chemistry, physiology or medicine, literature, economics and the promotion of peace. They are named after Swedish industrialist Alfred Nobel.

PHILISTINES
People who lived in ancient Palestine more than 3000 years ago. They were enemies of the Israelites and were defeated by King David.

PHILOSOPHER
A person who thinks extremely deeply about many subjects such as what it is to be a living human being, good and evil, religion and politics – and tries to understand and find out the truth behind these topics.

PROSE
The ordinary form of written language composed of phrases, sentences and paragraphs, rather than broken up into lines or verses, as in songs or poems.

ROBOT
A machine that carries out certain tasks according to human instructions. Some robots have human-like features and actions. Robots in factories carry out repetitive processes, usually controlled by computer.

SAGA
A medieval tale of Icelandic or Norwegian heroes and adventures. Modern-day sagas entail long and detailed stories about successive generations of the same family.

SATELLITE
An object that goes round, or orbits, another object. The Moon is the natural satellite of the Earth. Communications satellites also orbit the Earth but they are artificial (man-made).

SATIRE
The use of techniques such as jokes, clever wit, irony or sarcasm, to expose wrong-doing or stupidity, or to make fun of an individual.

SCRIPTURES
Sacred, solemn or authoritative pieces of writing, usually traditional and from ancient times. The collection of Christian literature known as the Bible is often called The Scriptures.

SCROLL
A long piece of paper or parchment (dried animal skin used like paper), with writing on it, which is rolled up for storage.

SLAVERY
The act of taking people's freedom away, and making them work hard for others against their will, for no money or rewards, but just to stay alive and be fed.

SPY
A person who pretends to be someone else, for example, who joins an enemy organization to find out information which can then be used against it.

THEORY
A set or system of ideas or proposals, which tries to explain how something works or happens. Theories are tested by observing and doing experiments, to find out if they are true.

TRADITION
The passing on of the culture of a group of people from old to young, including their customs, stories, history and beliefs.

TRAGEDY
A very sad event, such as an unhappy love affair, an appalling crime or a disaster. In theatre, the term refers to a play about a sequence of unhappy events which usually end for the worst.

TUBERCULOSIS (TB)
An infectious disease caused by tiny germs called bacteria, which produces small, round swellings or tubercles in the lungs, and symptoms such as terrible coughing, pain, weakness and breathing problems.

Index

ACKNOWLEDGEMENTS

Art Archive: Page 8 (t/r) Musée des Arts Décoratifs Paris/Dagli Orti, 11 (t/r) Archaeological Museum Filippi/Dagli Orti, 12 (t/r) Private Collection/Eileen Tweedy, (b/r) Art Archive, 14 (t/r) Victoria and Albert Museum London/Eileen Tweedy, 15 (c) Art Archive, 16 (t/r) Art Archive, 20 (t/r) The British Library, 21 (t/r) Musée du Château de Versailles/Dagli Orti, 22 (b/l) Civiche Racc d'Arte Moderna Pavia/Dagli Orti, 26 (t/r) Private Collection/Eileen Tweedy, (c/l) Courage Breweries/Eileen Tweedy **Corbis:** Page 16 (c/l) Bettmann, 23 (b) Archivo Iconografico, 25 (c) Robbie Jack, 32 (b/l) Historical Picture Archive, 33 (b/r) Hulton-Deutsch Collection, 35 (c/l) Charles E. Rotkin, (b) Joel W. Roger **Kobal:** Page 17 (t/r) Selznik Films, 18 (b) Paramount, 19 (b/r) EON / United Artists, 24 (b) UFA, 25 (t/r) Sparham, Laurie/Miramax Films/Universal Pictures, 29 (t/r) MGM, (c) Kobal Collection, 30 (t/r) Paramount, (c/l) 20th Century Fox, (b) Kobal Collection, 31 (c) MGM, (b/l) Umbrella/Rosenblum/Virgin Films, 33 (t/l) Distant Horizons/Miramax, (c/r) 20th Century Fox

The publishers would like to thank Anne Frank Stichting of the Anne Frank House for the use of photographic material.

All other photographs are from:
MKP Archives; Corel Corporation; Photodisk